Feelings

Worried

Sarah Medina

Illustrated by Jo Brooker

Heinemann Library
Chicago, Illinois

Customer Service 888–454–2279
Visit our website at www.heinemannlibrary.com

Photo research by Erica Martin
Designed by Jo Malivoire
Color Reproduction by Dot Gradations Ltd, UK
Printed in China by South China Printing Company Limited

12 11 10 09 08
10 9 8 7 6 5 4 3 2 1

Library of Congress Cataloging-in-Publication Data
Medina, Sarah, 1960-
  Worried / Sarah Medina; illustrated by Jo Brooker.
     p. cm. -- (Feelings)
  Includes bibliographical references and index.
  ISBN 978-1-4034-9796-3 (hc) -- ISBN 978-1-4034-9803-8 (pb)
  1. Worry--Juvenile literature. I. Brooker, Jo, 1957- II. Title.
  BF575.W8M43 2007
  152.4'6--dc22

                              200701545

Acknowledgments
The author and publisher are grateful to the following for permission to reproduce copyright material:
Bananastock p. **22 C, D**; Corbis p. **22A**; Getty Images/Taxi p. **22B**.

Contents

Some words are shown in bold, **like this**. They are explained in the glossary on page 23.

What Is Worry?

Worry is a **feeling**. Feelings are something you feel inside. Everyone has different feelings all the time.

happy

sad

angry

When you feel worried, you may think that something bad is going to happen.

What Happens When I Am Worried?

When you are worried, you may feel sick and have a **stomach ache.**

You might feel that your heart is **beating** very hard. You may not be able to sleep.

Why Do I Feel Worried?

You might feel worried when you do something for the first time, like start at a new school.

You may worry because you think that people will not play with you.

Is It Okay to Feel Worried?

Everybody feels worried sometimes.
Worry is not a nice **feeling**.

It is okay to worry sometimes, but don't worry too much. You may miss out on fun things!

What Can I Do If I Feel Worried?

If you are worried about something, tell someone who cares about you. They will help you.

Try not to think too much about what worries you. Play a game or do something fun instead.

Will I Always Feel Worried?

Feelings always change. You may feel
worried sometimes, but you will not

always worry.

When you feel worried, remember
the times when you were happy.

How Can I Tell If Someone Is Worried?

When people feel worried about something, they may not feel like eating their lunch.

They may not want to play with you. They might prefer to stay by themselves.

Can I Help When Someone Feels Worried?

When people feel worried, you can help them. Ask why they are worried. Listen to them carefully.

Tell them that you will help them, if you can. Or ask an adult for help.

I Feel Better Now!

Remember, everyone feels worried sometimes. Feeling worried is okay as long as you do not worry too much.

It is good to know what to do when you feel worried. Then you can think of what to do to feel better.

What Are These Feelings?

A

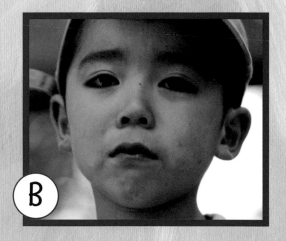

B

C

D

Which of these people look happy?

What are the other people feeling?

Look at page 24 to see the answers.

Picture Glossary

beating
making a sound or moving up and down in your chest

feeling
something that you feel inside. Worry is a feeling.

stomach ache
pain in your stomach

Index

Answers to the questions on page 22

The person in picture D looks happy. The other people could be worried, angry, or sad.

Note to Parents and Teachers

Reading for information is an important part of a child's literacy development. Learning begins with a question about something. Help children think of themselves as investigators and researchers by encouraging their questions about the world around them. Most chapters in this book begin with a question. Read the question together. Look at the pictures. Talk about what you think the answer might be. Then read the text to find out if your predictions were correct. Think of other questions you could ask about the topic, and discuss where you might find the answers. Assist children in using the picture glossary and the index to practice new vocabulary and research skills.